PRODUCTS: FROM IDEA TO MARKET

TVs

by Abby Doty

FOCUS READERS®
BEACON

www.focusreaders.com

Copyright © 2025 by Focus Readers®, Mendota Heights, MN 55120. All rights reserved. No part of this book may be reproduced or utilized in any form or by any means without written permission from the publisher.

Focus Readers is distributed by North Star Editions:
sales@northstareditions.com | 888-417-0195

Produced for Focus Readers by Red Line Editorial.

Photographs ©: Shutterstock Images, cover, 1, 6, 8, 11, 13, 16, 19, 21, 22, 25, 26, 29; iStockphoto, 4; AP Images, 15

Library of Congress Cataloging-in-Publication Data
Library of Congress Cataloging-in-Publication Data is available on the Library of Congress website.

ISBN
979-8-88998-408-5 (hardcover)
979-8-88998-436-8 (paperback)
979-8-88998-489-4 (ebook pdf)
979-8-88998-464-1 (hosted ebook)

Printed in the United States of America
Mankato, MN
012025

About the Author

Abby Doty is a writer, editor, and booklover from Minnesota.

Table of Contents

CHAPTER 1

Movie Night 5

CHAPTER 2

Making TVs Better 9

THAT'S AMAZING!

Then and Now 14

CHAPTER 3

Building TVs 17

CHAPTER 4

Buying TVs 23

Focus Questions • 28

Glossary • 30

To Learn More • 31

Index • 32

CHAPTER 1

Movie Night

A girl and her family sit down on their couch. They hold bowls of popcorn. The girl dims the lights. Then she grabs the remote. The family is ready for movie night.

 Every year, more than 40 million TVs are sold in the United States.

Good TVs show clear images from close up and far away.

The family just bought a new television. Their old TV showed blurry images. And the sound was hard to hear. The new TV is much bigger. It is also thinner.

The movie begins playing. The girl watches the TV closely. The images are bright and colorful. She sees the characters on screen moving smoothly. The sound is clear, too. She loves watching. She wonders how someone made the TV.

Did You Know?

In 2023, the average TV screen was 50 inches (127 cm). But some TVs are hundreds of inches across.

CHAPTER 2

Making TVs Better

Many types of TVs exist. But companies still come up with new ideas. They want to keep creating better TVs. To do this, companies may use new materials. And they may try new technology.

Some TV screens are curved. That makes images seem bigger and brighter.

For example, companies want their screens to show the clearest images. So, they create screens with more **pixels**.

Businesses also listen to customers' ideas. Companies use those ideas to create new TVs. For example, many people want to use streaming services on their TVs.

Did You Know?

Many TVs have millions of pixels. Some have more than 33 million.

In the 2020s, most TVs in US homes were smart TVs.

So, companies make **smart** TVs. These TVs can connect to the internet. Other customers may want lighter TVs. Companies can use thinner parts and smaller controls in their TVs. That results in a lighter product.

Companies think about all these possibilities. They gather ideas. Then it is time to make their new TVs. Video and sound scientists work together. They create designs. Then the teams create **prototypes**.

When a prototype is ready, people test it. They use different tools to check its parts. Some tests check the sound system. They listen to how well the speakers work. Other tests check the images. The screen should be bright and clear.

Technicians may do small fixes on TV prototypes.

Teams collect information from these tests. They use it to make improvements. Once the TV design is perfect, the company can start producing lots of them.

THAT'S AMAZING!

Then and Now

In the 1920s, John Logie Baird created the first TV. The screen was only a few inches tall. A few years later, the **electronic** TV was created. This type of TV began to spread. At first, the TVs were expensive. Only wealthy people could buy them. But soon, TVs got cheaper. By the 1950s, many people owned them.

TVs have changed a lot over the years. Most early TVs were big and heavy. In the 2000s, flat-screen TVs became popular. These TVs weighed less. Their screens were bigger and clearer.

By the 1960s, most US households had TVs.

CHAPTER 3

Building TVs

TVs are built in factories. Workers and machines put TVs together. Getting materials is the first step. TVs use lots of glass. They also include plastic and metal. Several different **minerals** are needed, too.

Workers put together some parts of TVs by hand.

17

All these materials are shipped to factories.

Most TVs have four main parts. Machines help create them. One part is the TV's plastic frame. Another part is the sound system. That includes speakers and wires. TVs also have electronic pieces inside. These pieces power the TVs and control them.

The last main part is the TV screen. Many modern TVs use LCD screens. *LCD* stands for "liquid

Wires and plugs on TVs help people watch and listen to different content.

crystal display." LCD screens include two sheets of glass. One catches **electrical signals**. It uses liquid crystal material. The other sheet has different kinds of pixels.

They help create the color of the images. Both sheets are formed in factories. Then the sheets are joined together.

Other details are added in factories, too. For example, **LED** lights help LCD screens look better. They make the images brighter and clearer. They also use less power.

Did You Know?

People purchase hundreds of millions of LCD TVs each year.

Factory workers test screens to make sure they work well.

Finally, the TVs are complete. Workers check the sound, screens, and more. Then, workers package the TVs up. After that, it is time to ship them off. Customers can buy the finished TVs.

CHAPTER 4

Buying TVs

Customers can buy TVs in many ways. Some purchase TVs online. Others visit stores in person. Customers have a lot of options. So, companies must stand out. They need to **advertise** their TVs.

Stores display TVs of different types, sizes, and brands.

23

That can convince buyers to choose a specific company's TVs.

Many businesses advertise with **commercials**. These ads show why their TVs are the best. For example, the ads may show a TV's clear images. They could describe how good the sound is. Many buyers care about these qualities.

Other ads may focus on a TV's price. TVs that cost less can reach more buyers. For many people, price is the most important part.

People often upgrade their TV every five to seven years.

They may pick cheap TVs instead of TVs with many features.

Often, TV ads target certain groups. Internet connection may be important to young customers. Older buyers may focus on size.

25

Gamers might want big screens to play on.

Large-screen TVs help them see more easily. Some TVs have extra connecting points for gaming machines. Customers who enjoy playing video games may want that feature.

Partnerships can help companies find buyers, too. A TV company may team up with a streaming or gaming service. Customers can get a TV and service at the same time. Buyers may like that deal. That helps the business make more money. And customers are happy with their TVs.

Did You Know?

Many companies let customers return TVs if they are not happy.

Focus Questions

Write your answers on a separate piece of paper.

1. Write a few sentences explaining the main ideas of Chapter 2.

2. What features of a TV are the most important to you? Why?

3. When was the first TV created?
   - **A.** 1920s
   - **B.** 1960s
   - **C.** 2000s

4. Why might companies advertise to certain groups of people?
   - **A.** All customers want the same TV.
   - **B.** Customers may want different kinds of TVs.
   - **C.** Companies want fewer customers to buy TVs.

5. What does **partnerships** mean in this book?

Partnerships can help companies find buyers, too. A TV company may team up with a streaming or gaming service.

- **A.** when companies do everything alone
- **B.** when companies give away free things
- **C.** when companies work together

6. What does **target** mean in this book?

*Often, TV ads **target** certain groups. Internet connection may be important to young customers. Older buyers may focus on size.*

- **A.** hide from
- **B.** ignore customers
- **C.** aim messages at

Answer key on page 32.

Glossary

advertise
To make messages or videos about a product so customers want to buy it.

commercials
Messages or videos to sell a product. They appear during other programs.

electrical signals
Ways of sending information by electricity.

electronic
Powered by electricity.

LED
LED stands for light-emitting diode. LED devices give off light when electricity goes through them.

minerals
Substances that form naturally under the ground.

pixels
Tiny lit-up squares on a screen that make up an image.

prototypes
Early forms of something, usually for testing.

smart
Able to connect to the internet.

To Learn More

BOOKS

Amstutz, Lisa J. *Before Television*. Mendota Heights, MN: Focus Readers, 2020.

Martin, Emmett. *Everything Is Streaming: Music, Movies, and More*. New York: Gareth Stevens Publishing, 2023.

Ungvarsky, Janine. *Inventing Televisions*. Mendota Heights, MN: Focus Readers, 2022.

NOTE TO EDUCATORS

Visit **www.focusreaders.com** to find lesson plans, activities, links, and other resources related to this title.

Index

A
advertising, 23–25

B
Baird, John Logie, 14

C
commercials, 24
customers, 10–11, 21, 23, 25–27

D
designs, 12–13

E
electrical signals, 19
electronic TVs, 14

F
factories, 17–18, 20

I
internet, 11, 25

L
LCD screens, 18–20
LED lights, 20

M
materials, 9, 17–19
minerals, 17

P
partnerships, 27
pixels, 10, 19
prototypes, 12

S
scientists, 12
screens, 7, 10, 12, 14, 18–21, 26
smart TVs, 11
sound system, 12, 18

T
technology, 9
tests, 12–13

Answer Key: 1. Answers will vary. 2. Answers will vary. 3. A; 4. B; 5. C; 6. C